POETRY

September 2017

FOUNDED IN 1912 BY HARRIET MONROE

VOLUME CCX · NUMBER 5

CONTENTS

September 2017

POEMS

FROM AN OPEN MAP: THE CORRESPONDENCE OF ROBERT DUNCAN AND CHARLES OLSON

Editor	DON SHARE
Art Director	FRED SASAKI
Associate Editor	LINDSAY GARBUTT
Assistant Editor	HOLLY AMOS
Marketing & Production Assistant	HANNAH KUCHARZAK
Consulting Editor	CHRISTINA PUGH
Design	ALEXANDER KNOWLTON
Design Consultant	PENTAGRAM

POETRYMAGAZINE.ORG

A PUBLICATION OF THE
POETRY FOUNDATION
PRINTED BY CADMUS PROFESSIONAL COMMUNICATIONS, US

Poetry · September 2017 · Volume 210 · Number 5

POEMS

MICHAEL HOFMANN

Sankt Georg

Sankt Georg, what was it, questionable, doubtful, shady, twilit,
a something area, something Jan said, and he was born in Hamburg,
and went to school here, so he would know.

A little isthmus between the Alster with its freshwater sailors
and the railway station, always a reliable drag on things anywhere in
    Europe
(the transients, the drugs, the preset collisions between the foolish
    young

and the unscrupulous old), though this one piped classical music —
    not anymore —
to the forecourt, where taxi drivers got out
and walked their Mercs around in neutral

because they were hours without a fare and were saving diesel
(which was all very well in summer),
and the immediate, somehow always slightly grubby or compromised
    view

of three theatres, two museums, and le Carré's bunker hotel,
but, hey, it was classy while it lasted,
and you could get to Milan or Moscow if you had to.

Then the *Polizeibezirk* of underage *Puppenstrich* about the time
B. came here from the country,
still often the only girl not on the game, among whores

and winos and people "with an immigration background"
looking grim and wearing subfusc and doing the messages, as we
    once said. Then gays —
is there a pink euro, like a pink pound, and the Pink Pistols and gray
    wolves? —

intrepid advance guard of gentrification.
So up the rents, send in the heavies, firebomb the buildings, locals
    out,
make improvements, and up the rents again, same everywhere.

A natty pellucid pissoir in the Hanser Platz that it would take Paris
    to pull off,
drunks round the monument ("reel around the fountain"), hardy
    trees and hardier women,
little roosters, little rosters in the apartment block for cleaning the
    common parts,

little brass squares set in the ground for individual fascist outrages,
with the victims' names, the massy church at the end of the street —
St. George's, the AIDS church, the rainbow flag,

the incendiary community paper called the *Dragon*.
Sudden sad flurries of flowers, the curt pairs of dates,
a grown-out bleached person with one leg.

The main drag changed utterly,
meaning as usual stylistic *diktat* from elsewhere
and the birth of an interchangeably frippish hideousness. Three hat
    shops,

an empty tea bar (tax write-off? money laundry?) boasting sixteen
    varieties of macaroons,
endless places to stop (if you even wanted to stop) on the narrow
    pavement
between the heedless cars and the nosy passersby,

expensive ready-cooked food shops with names like *Mom's*, gone
the hardware store that stocked everything and was staffed by
    people
who advised you where to find it for even less, out of business,

or moved away to less promising parts.
The photo shops, the record store, bookshop. All gone.
And behind that, the Steindamm, our belly and balls,

twinned with Kabul, or Mombasa, or Abuja.
Telephone shops if you wanted to call anywhere with a red, green,
    and black flag
(launch pad of Ali Ağca and his crew of martyrs), casinos,

thorny or hairy vegetables, fetish stores, Alphonso mangoes from
    Pakistan,
video brothels, limitless mint and parsley and cilantro, hourly hotels,
cracked olives and fresh cheese, old girls with three words of
    German, newly baked flatbread.

The birds strike up between three and four (it's the Northern light),
while at lit intersections they never stop.
Twilit, doubtful, shady, something. Questionable.

Valais

A working river, a working valley,
The gray-green Rhône
Lined with workings, heaps of dust, gravel, cement,
And logjams waiting for transport,
Like the island exporting itself to its neighbors one barge at a time.

The river, the road, and the railway,
A plait, a tangle, a place of through.
The river not navigable, the boggy valley floor not walkable,
The locals came down from the mountains a little way
To site castles on moraine and regulate trade.

Hannibal marched his elephants through here, dynamited rocks
    with vinegar.
Poplars were planted en passant by Napoleon's *Grande Armée*
Two-hundred-some years ago.
Goethe came to visit.
The shade endures.

Rilke was reminded of Spain.
He lived among apricots at Muzot,
Just the other side of the language barrier,
And fixed to be buried with a view of France.
No one knows who I am, were his dying words.

Smells of hay and dung, the murmurs of subtle conversation
Next door are tax-efficient sheep
The underground chicken palace like CERN
Or a discreet gun emplacement.
The lights come on when we appear, and go off after we're gone.

Larchwood and rye bread, chocolate and slate,
Dried beef and stone
All one striated substance,

The staff of life breaking explosively, crumblingly,
If it breaks at all,

A stash of daunting verticals,
A washing machine delivered by helicopter
Winched down into the Renaissance casbah.
Time was a man had to carry his donkey across his shoulders up a
    cliff;
Now everything is tunnel fodder.

Electricity and water come piped through the mountains,
The vineyards get a sousing under great rainbow arcs,
Who wouldn't want to die in a thirteenth-century tower
With light sensors and cold running water
Off the hills and a chill in the sunny air of the contemporary archaic.

Nocturne

Yes, your face like asphalt dust on my tongue
whenever it rains. I'll say it's the last time I call,
        tomorrow. In your arms it won't be the same,
each step farther from the border. Gin and tonics.
        Tequila grapefruits. I threw that black mug
at your face after gin, after tequila, I didn't know
        Enrique's Journey would trigger me,
I'm sorry. I drank too much. I drink too much,
        yes, I know. It wasn't me who threw it,
I said, but it was. It's me who needs to learn
        how to face grandpa's bullet shells,
bottles, broken chairs, doors he woke us up with.
        I was four. I saw Mom between his gun
and Grandma. I was four. I need to forgive
        the coins he placed in my hands
to buy him vodka. Grandpa chased every single
        one of his daughters with his machete
in the middle of the day, in the middle of the night,
        I didn't know what to do except climb
the water tower across the street with Red Power Ranger.
        He's chased us to this country
that trained him to stay quiet when "his boss"
        put prisoners in black bags, then pushed them
out the truck, "for everyone to see what happens
        to bad people here." Gin, straight up.
Tequila shots. I've picked up the shards in our apartment,
        wiped the black smudge next to our bed,
promised never to do it again, that I'll seek help,
        but I don't. I make an excuse. No one understands
why Abuelita never left him. It's mid-June,
        Venus and Mars the closest they've been
in 2,000 years, but I've never seen grandparents hug,
        or hold hands. I make an excuse.
You kept rubbing your hands. When I turned six
        grandpa quit drinking. He stayed at home

at night but never talked to us. He didn't like gin.
Didn't like writers. Didn't like leftists.
Everyone gone except one aunt. You're not here.
Tomorrow, tampoco. These walls snore
like grandpa's slurred shouts. I thought the border
would take him. All my aunts,
my mom, thought so too. We're all running
from the sun on his machete.
The moon on his gun.

Gloves

How long can you speak.
Without inhaling. How long.
Can you inhale without.
Bursting apart. History is wagging.
Its ass at us. Twirling in its silver.
Cape. I want to kiss.
Your scalp. I want you to kiss.
My friends. Can you see the wet.
Azalea quivering.
On its vine. Its ripening.
Dread. If it never rained again.
I would still wear.
My coat. Still wrap.
My socks in plastic. Doing.
One thing is a way.
Of not doing everything else.
Today I answer only.
To my war name. Wise.
Salt. I can make.
A stone float off into.
The sky. I can make.
A whole family.
Disappear. I know.
So many people.
Have been awful to you.
I've given each one.
A number. When you're ready.
I will ask you to draw me.
Their hands.

Waiting for the Twelfth

In Shia Islam, the Twelfth Imam is said to have disappeared in the ninth century.
It's believed his return at the end of the world will deliver order from the chaos.

no one ever brings up the wages
of virtue   the cost of avoiding

that which you were built
to do   some men actually love

their enemies   remind me to tell you
about them when you arrive and

when will that be again?   I've already
spiced the duck and hidden

the sherry   even grain has
genes that say *drink this* or *bend*

there so much like our
own   I am rubbing yogurt

through my hair getting ready
for your return   I read old

mail from my bababazorg
the Farsi like tea leaves

or exotic blades   years
ago he melted into the tautness

of earth like a pad of butter on
turtle meat   the birch

curled its tongue   I was full of
credible fears   today I'm full

of olives and smoke   sucking
a fat red cigar and ashing on

the good lace   I'm comfy
as a snake sleeping in

a silk shoe though my glasses
are foggy or maybe I just got

perfume in my eye   either
way I'll recognize you

by your heartbeat you'll
recognize me by the green

bird in my shirt pocket   if you
hurry I'll let you hold

her   her flightlessness
will mean nothing in fact

my whole house has been
cleansed entirely of

symbols   a strange
call came from the west

and I understood it in
this new language   I burnt

away my candles and woke the
sleeping spider resting his fangs

against my hand   there will be
nothing here to distract you

from your work   just
some old pears

browning in the kitchen
and a glass vase

of pink roses
humming their little songs

ROY G. GUZMÁN

Those Seventy-Two Bodies Belong to Us

After the 2010 San Fernando massacre
Para Luis

You novelize a route with flesh dumped at the ranch, can't backtrack
the courage of miles we traversed in the dark, on a sighing speedboat,

through jungles that spat only shoes, calzones, bodies twisted
as guitarras when there's no grito left in them to pluck. Back home,

we priested our mornings with sun-dried sombreros, communed
with our ghosts & had no wish to sacrifice our bellies, our terneros,

our Consuelos. With wings from acero, we'd crash latitudinal
     objections,
mystify Bengay on the mouths of our map-torn feet, pay no heed

to grief's ambidextrous strophes. If we choked on our own blood
we harpooned optimism. But when the vans deadlocked our
     pilgrimage

we knew our shadows had crumbed the anesthetic vultures.
They pressed their loaded beaks upon our backs until our knees bent

sour orange. One asked if we served the enemy, but we took enemy
to mean a seed that sits quietly underfoot, abashed to vestibule

the grating sun. Blindfolded, we faced the gloom volcanoes
of their mothers. How those mothers might've screamed like ours

in their tortured independence: bloody thunder in the brown-
     starched
symphonies, a wind that howled & shoved its thumbs through feral
     lands

probing for judgment or commiseration. Chingado god that copy-
    catted
these legs from monotony. Chingado god that hewed our wrists,

a pair of stems to strap behind our wrested boots & jeans. Whoever
supplied a plea to that deviant afternoon's rationed blessings

neglected to add chile, sazón, a nosegay of tortillas to the long road.
Mothers who've come to reclaim our tongues in the dirt: remind us

of the braids in the phrasings of our dreams before we vanished. Pat
the ground for the bodkinned orchids. Wasn't it yesterday we were

siphoning forecasts with our fingers roving on the table? Or caught
your chests pain-leavened & stilled them with the rumpus of our
    hopes?

TERRANCE HAYES

American Sonnet for My Past and Future Assassin

I lock you in an American sonnet that is part prison,
Part panic closet, a little room in a house set aflame.
I lock you in a form that is part music box, part meat
Grinder to separate the song of the bird from the bone.
I lock your persona in a dream-inducing sleeper hold
While your better selves watch from the bleachers.
I make you both gym & crow here. As the crow
You undergo a beautiful catharsis trapped one night
In the shadows of the gym. As the gym, the feel of crow-
Shit dropping to your floors is not unlike the stars
Falling from the pep rally posters on your walls.
I make you a box of darkness with a bird in its heart.
Voltas of acoustics, instinct & metaphor. It is not enough
To love you. It is not enough to want you destroyed.

American Sonnet for My Past and Future Assassin

Probably twilight makes blackness dangerous
Darkness. Probably all my encounters
Are existential jambalaya. Which is to say,
A nigga can survive. Something happened
In Sanford, something happened in Ferguson
And Brooklyn & Charleston, something happened
In Chicago & Cleveland & Baltimore & happens
Almost everywhere in this country every day.
Probably someone is prey in all of our encounters.
You won't admit it. The names alive are like the names
In graves. Probably twilight makes blackness
Darkness. And a gate. Probably the dark blue skin
Of a black man matches the dark blue skin
Of his son the way one twilight matches another.

American Sonnet for My Past and Future Assassin

Why are you bugging me you stank minuscule husk
Of musk, muster & deliberation crawling over reasons
And possessions I have & have not touched?
Should I fail in my insecticide, I pray for a black boy
Who lifts you to a flame with bedeviled tweezers
Until mercy rises & disappears. You are the size
Of a stuttering drop of liquid — milk, machine oil,
Semen, blood. Yes, you funky stud, you are the jewel
In the knob of an elegant butt plug, snug between
Pleasure & disgust. You are the scent of rot at the heart
Of lovemaking. The meat inside your exoskeleton
Is as tender as Jesus. Neruda wrote of "a nipple
Perfuming the earth." Yes, you are an odor, an almost
Imperceptible ode to death, a lousy, stinking stinkbug.

American Sonnet for My Past and Future Assassin

Inside me is a black-eyed animal
Bracing in a small stall. As if a bird
Could grow without breaking its shell.
As if the clatter of a thousand black
Birds whipping in a storm could be held
In a shell. Inside me is a huge black
Bull balled small enough to fit inside
The bead of a nipple ring. I mean to leave
A record of my raptures. I was raised
By a beautiful man. I loved his grasp of time.
My mother shaped my grasp of space.
Would you rather spend the rest of eternity
With your wild wings bewildering a cage or
With your four good feet stuck in a plot of dirt?

ELIZABETH METZGER

Inmate of Happiness

Because you were born with your knees
tied together under you
you are bound to need your hands
and resent my knees. Because

you were born with and without knees
your face remains close to the ground
to analyze all the methods
the medics use to unhook them:

they splint your legs against planks,
numb each knee with a balm
that makes you feel you are flying
through stone. Now you crouch

ready to doubt, blinking because
it is your body's to blink.
You smile, invincibly obscured.
From any closer I couldn't take you whole

so you imagine your hands luring
my knees into both sides of your mouth
and open your smile
into a needy room — molded

behind your teeth, a person of pity
held down in thick liquid shame.
Because you were born to be happy
you would skin and uncap

the knee of a good giant
to make yourself a helmet
that could guard you from under
the brain, but you cannot get up off those knees.

ATSURO RILEY

Creekthroat

— We seen his mama she dry and scant

By hook or by bent
I guttle the rudimental stories.

I'm all in-scoop
suck and swallow by dint of birth.   Of shape.

— Were *you* hallow-nursed on riversource
upon a time (or *'the rocky breasts forever'*) I was not.

I learned to lie in want
for succor-food; for forms; I lunged I gulped for what I got.

Nowadays to need
to come by what comes by here comes natural and needs no bait.

Just steep dead-still as a blacksnake
creek and wait.

> [*my chokesome weeds, my crook, my lack, my epiphytes*
> *my cypress knees ...*]

This old appetite as chronic as tides —
on foot or by boat by night (*please*) come slake me with radicle stories.

Knell

We low on daddies hereabouts

The fathers all but gone

Our lack a weight

a shape a drybone lake

By war by

drink by

gun by

drift

The father's all but gone.

Element

— Way on back through the underwood by Bowen's Canal

Well we'd heard it to be veiny with cottonmouths I'm not gonna lie.

•

For true
the sheer (snake-electric) back-beyond of the place
put a pull on us like a magnet.

•

That that rag-rope (flagged and) barred the path just egged us on.

•

(To go and
skulk- and sidle-learn
to palp and tap the edge
to crack us in.)

•

— What'd we feel there once we'd crossed?

•

Veritable
thought-thick trunks
of swampfoot oaks.

•

Something like *'a shift in the structure of experience.'*

•

Here was
Johnny Pep (shrapped home from war)
branch-dragging
agglomerating discards and disjecta.

•

His craving wove a plexus (more a house) from limbs and leaves.

•

He knit us in:
he left us be.   He let us watch he watched us try
(to climb to ape his crisscross weave)
to pitch to plait the roof.

•

Something like '*Yall strayboys welcome to be welcome if you work.*'

•

Didn't we 'work' —
particular night-hoots (and near-chromatic whistle-riffs) in echo;
    likenesses
he whittled live from hickory showed us how.

•

He'd let us
watch him strip and shave
the shagbark bark
to taste (to read) to mull the grain.

•

Something like '*root-room*' I reckon.   Something like

•

'*When Johnny Pep hitched home from war*
                    we took to carving (curing) scraplings into shapes.'

Milk

His mother

came (she said) from salt

so fed him salt.

Raised to wolf

white roots and dirt

she fed him dirt.

Lobe

The coarse croker-sack cloth

she'd grown to clutch

mesh-merged with her

woof and pang

rose to serve

more like organ

than protection

ROSANNA WARREN

The Mink

When the mink ran across the meadow in bunched
black parabolas, I thought
sine and cosine, but no —
the movement never dips
below the line. The creature vanished
into barberries. Absolute
predator who cracks a rabbit's spine
in one bite. And my mind

leapt along a track to a summer field
where I walked years ago
to a stony spit out into the North Atlantic
with a young man I hardly knew, and his sister.
He was bald, dying
of a brain tumor. I ignored
his illness and we spoke of history.
He was gentle, scholarly. Why

do I remember him
when it was his sister I painted seated in tall grass,
her forehead wide, brown hair framing her face,
ocean a cobalt swatch behind?
Islands humped in little arcs across the bay.
That canvas is stacked in a closet.
But it's the dead boy
I've stored inside me all these years,

scared of the otherworldly light
around his eyes. Scared and ashamed
of what I didn't know. Ashamed of my fear
that made his death, when it came,
unspeakable. So history bounds
into the present, glitter-eyed, with musky anal glands
and daggering eyeteeth. Because that boy
wasn't dead: he must be killed again.

DANA ROESER

Transparent Things, God-Sized Hole

All transparent things need
        thunder shirts. The little
ghost hanging from an eave,
        on Underwood
Street, a piece of
        lavender-tinted
netting stretched onto
        a metal frame. The Boston
terriers and Chihuahuas patiently
        wait out storms
with their eyes bulging
        in their special
wraparound shirts. My
        family used to
laugh at me
        sleeping under
two down quilts, wearing a wool
        hat in summer,
when I said
        I was afraid
otherwise I would
        fly up to the ceiling.

Once on a sidewalk
        beside Erie Street
around the corner
        from Underwood
where the pointless
        obsolete
tracks run to a dead end
        on the other side,
I found a black
        and silver rosary,
with shining
        onyx beads, like

the ones
            that you see
hanging
            from the belts of
nuns in their habits or priests
            in their chasubles.
I kept it
            carefully until either
I lost it or it got buried
            in the bottom of a purse
abandoned under
            my bed or in the
closet. Clutter keeps
            me bound to
this earth.
                  I told Patti last night
            that the God-sized
hole in me was
            so big and vacant,
voracious and spacious,
            it was like I was
running some kind
            of desperate toddler's
shape-sorter game, trying to find
            something that fit
to plug into it. I'd stuff anything
            in there, regardless
of whether the shape
            coincided with
the opening. It was
            like I could look
at the sky and attract
            space junk, broken
satellites, spent rocket
            stages,

micrometeoroids, to
    plug the
gap.

    The wind is its own
kind of chaos,
        sometimes like a sheet
of itself tangled
        or flowing
on a celestial
        clothesline. It needs
a weighted blanket.
        Little red flags
on the maple
        at the corner of
Underwood and Erie
        near the switching yard.
Slow-moving locomotives
        that might be driven by
nobody. Flags
        hold the tree down,
mark it, make it know
        it's real.
Flapping on the flaming maple
        or falling.

Girls Online

The first line is a row of girls,
twenty-five of them, almost
a painting, shoulders overlapping,
angled slightly toward you.
One says: *I'm myself here.*
The others shudder and laugh
through the ribbon core that strings
them. They make a tone tighter
by drumming on their thighs and
opening their mouths. The girls
are cells. The girls are a fence,
a fibrous network. One by one
they describe their grievances.
Large hot malfunctioning
machines lie obediently at their sides.
Their shirts are various shades
of ease in the surrounding air,
which is littered with small cuts.
One will choose you, press you
into the ground. You may never
recover. The second-to-last line
has a fold in it. The last line is
the steady pour of their names.

COLE SWENSEN

Luigi Galvani 1737–1798

married a woman who was perfectly happy
                                    to turn half their apartment
into a laboratory
                    including the cadavers necessary to her husband's
explorations in surgery.
                        He also wrote articles on the ears of birds and
in Latin, an anatomist, standing motionless
                                            in the middle of the road
                            thinking
that electricity must activate the blood
                                    while the muscles, themselves
living Leyden jars, flowered among
                                those who found it difficult
to believe that electricity is an animal
                                lost in a garden of showering towers
and, as with all living things, a certain degree
                                    of the domestic filtered down
between his hands to land
                        in a dusting of involuntary silver across
the surface of every nerve.

André-Marie Ampère 1775–1836

electrically rowed Rousseau from a wide green meadow

                                into his brain

along with Buffon and Diderot

                  and the entire Enlightenment embroidered

in fractions, thus confusing

                  poetry and mathematics. He stood back

and declared:

            An umbrella could envelope

                      a good part

of the village of Poleymieux en route to reviving the library

                          and why

did my wife die so young?

                Wrote out the psalms on his palm in the

electrodynamic molecules of his time

                  which he carried next to his heart

in a heart-shaped box

            obsessed

                  by Ørsted's magnetized needle, leaping

full-grown and fully armed

                into the periodic table. Noble metals

isolated and at war

            put each order in order

                  and was the first to define

electric current as a circulation

            gazing out over the Mediterranean until it dies.

Hans Christian Ørsted 1777–1851

saw the magnet grow electric
                    and the fixed points
become a field in rural Denmark
                    as the needle moved through various materials
all the while remaining parallel:
                          the usual: silver, zinc, lead, etc.
and then tried needles of glass
                    needles of shellac
                          with all the west above
while below, the east in winding spirals
                      traveling three years across Europe,
a good friend of Hans Christian Andersen
                    and of aluminum, whose name points
to its invisible lights
            within
                  whose forces crossed and became
his galvanic opus, *The Soul in Nature*,
                    as well as various Italian newspapers —
to eventually end up as a park in Copenhagen
                    dominated by green, a lake, and shade
in which a woman dressed in green sits reading to this day.

ROBIN MORGAN
───────────

The Ghost Light

Lit from within is the sole secure way
to traverse dark matter. Some life forms —
certain mushrooms, snails, jellyfish, worms —
glow bioluminescent, and people as well; we
emit infrared light from our most lucent selves.
Our tragedy is we can't see it.

We see by reflection. We need biofluorescence
to show our true colors. External illumination can
distort, though. When gravity bends light, huge galaxy
clusters can act as telescopes, elongating background
images of star systems to faint arcs — a lensing effect
like viewing distant street lamps through a glass of wine.

A glass of wine or two now makes me weave
as if acting a drunkard's part; as if, besotted
with unrequited love for the dynamic Turner
canvases spied out by the Hubble, I could lurch
down a city street set without provoking
every pedestrian walk-on stare.

Stare as long as you need to. If you think about it,
walking, even standing, is illogical — such tiny things,
feet! — especially when one's body is not *al dente*
anymore. Besides, creature of extremes and excess,
I've always thought Apollo beautiful but boring,
a bit of a dumb blonde. Dionysians don't do balance.

Balance, in other words, has never been
my strong point. But I digress. More
and more these days, digression
seems the most direct route through
from where I've lost or found myself
out of place, mind, turn, time.

Place your foot just so, mind how you turn:
too swift a swivel can bring you down. Take your time
ushering the audience out, saying goodbye
to the actors. The ghost light
is what they call the single bulb hanging
above the bare stage in an empty theater.

In the empty theater of such a night, waking to meet
no external radiance, this is the final struggle left to win,
this the sole beacon to beckon the darkness in and let the rest
begin, this the lens through which at last to see both Self
and Other arrayed with the bright stain of original sin:
lit from within.

JOY HARJO

Tobacco Origin Story, Because Tobacco Was a Gift Intended to Walk Alongside Us to the Stars

From a story of how the tobacco plant came to our people,
told to me by my cousin George Coser Jr.

It was way back, before there was a way back
When time threaded earth and sky.
Children were conceived, were born, grew, and walked tall
In what we now call a day.
There must have been two suns, a bright moon, somehow
We had more light than now, sheen
Of falling in love playing about Earth's body
In a wild flicker which lit
Us up. We who were this planet and yearned for touch.
Every planted thought grew plant
Ladders to the stars, way back, before there was
No way back, *Miss Mary Mack.*
We used to sing along the buttons of her
Dress. Our babies are always
Our babies. Even back then when time waved through
The corn. We knew our plants like
Relatives. Their stories were our stories, there
Were songs for everything — I
Should say "are" songs for every transformation
They link between way back and
Now, the forever now, a time when a young
Mvskoke man and woman
Walked through the shimmer of the early evening.
They had become as one song.
They lay down when it was dark. I can hear their
Intimate low-voice talking.
How they tease one another with such gut love.
Earth makes a bed, with pillow
Mounds. And it is there as the night insects sing
They conceived their first child. They
Will look back as they walk East toward the sunrise.

The raw stalks of beginning
Will drink the light, root deeply dark into earth.
In the tracks of their loving
The plant-child emerges, first the seed head, then
Leafy, long male body and the white female
Flowers of tobacco, or
Hece, as the people called it when it called
To them. *Come here. We were brought*
To you from those who love you. We will help you.
And that's how it began, way
Back, when we knew how to hear the songs of plants
And could sing back, like now
On paper, with marks like bird feet, but where are
Our ears? They have grown to fit
Around earbuds, to hear music made for cold
Cash, like our beloved smoke-
Making threaded with addiction and dead words.
Sing this song back to me, girl.
In the moonlight, tobacco plant had silver
Moon buttons all up her back.
We're getting dressed to go plant new songs with words.
Our sun is dimming faster.
Mvto hece, mvto hvse, mvto e —
Kanvchaga, mvto ah

Redbird Love

We watched her grow up.
She was the urgent chirper,
Fledgling flier.
And when spring rolled
Out its green
She'd grown
Into the most noticeable
Bird-girl.
Long-legged and just
The right amount of blush
Tipping her wings, crest
And tail, and
She knew it
In the bird parade.
We watched her strut.
She owned her stuff.
The males perked their armor, greased their wings,
And flew sky-loop missions
To show off
For her.
In the end
There was only one.
Isn't that how it is for all of us?
There's that one you circle back to — for home.
This morning
The young couple scavenges seeds
On the patio.
She is thickening with eggs.
Their minds are busy with sticks the perfect size, tufts of fluff
Like dandelion, and other pieces of soft.
He steps aside for her, so she can eat.
Then we watch him fill his beak
Walk tenderly to her and kiss her with seed.
The sacred world lifts up its head

To notice —
We are double-, triple-blessed.

How to Write a Poem in a Time of War

You can't begin just anywhere. It's a wreck.

                                        Shrapnel and the eye

Of a house, a row of houses. There's a rat scrambling

From light with fleshy trash in its mouth. A baby strapped to its
  mother's back

Cut loose.   Soldiers crawl the city,

The river, the town, the village,

                        The bedroom, our kitchen. They eat everything.
Or burn it.

They kill what they cannot take. They rape. What they cannot kill
  they take.

Rumors fall like rain.

                Like bombs.

        Like mother and father tears swallowed for restless peace.

                        Like sunset slanting toward a moonless midnight.

Like a train blown free of its destination.   Like a seed fallen where

There is no chance of trees   or anyplace   for birds to live.

No, start here.   *Deer peer from the edge of the woods.*

We used to see woodpeckers

The size of the sun, redbirds, and were greeted

By chickadees with their good morning songs.

We'd started to cook outside slippery with dew and laughter, ah
those smoky sweet sunrises.

We tried to pretend war wasn't going to happen.

Though they began building their houses all around us and demanding
more.

They started teaching our children their god's story,

A story in which we'd always be slaves.

No. Not here.

You can't begin here.

*This is memory shredded because it is impossible to hold by words, even
poetry.*

These memories were left here with the trees:

The torn pocket of your daughter's hand-sewn dress,

The sash, the lace.

The baby's delicately beaded moccasin still connected to the foot,

A young man's note of promise to his beloved —

No! This is not the best place to begin.

Everyone was asleep, despite the distant bombs. Terror had become
the familiar stranger.

Our beloved twin girls curled up in their nightgowns, next to their
father and me.

If we begin here, none of us will make it to the end

Of the poem.

Someone has to make it out alive, sang a grandfather to his grandson,

His granddaughter, as he blew his most powerful song into the
hearts of the children.

There it would be hidden from the soldiers,

Who would take them miles, rivers, mountains from the navel cord
place

Of the origin story.

He knew one day, far day, the grandchildren would return,
generations later

Over slick highways   constructed over old trails

Through walls of laws meant to hamper or destroy, over the
libraries of

The ancestors in the winds, born in stones.

His song brings us to his home place in these smoky hills.

Begin here.

Becoming Seventy

Knoxville, December 27, 2016, for Marilyn Kallet's 70th birthday.
This poem was constructed to carry any memory you want to hold close.

We

arrived

when the days

grew legs of night.

Chocolates were offered.

We ate latkes for hours

to celebrate light and friends.

We will keep going despite dark

or a madman in a white house dream.

Let's talk about something else said the dog

who begs faithfully at the door of goodwill:

a biscuit will do, a voice of reason, meat sticks —

I dreamed all of this I told her, you, me, and Paris —

it was impossible to make it through the tragedy

without poetry. What are we without winds becoming words?

Becoming old children born to children born to sing us into

love. Another level of love, beyond the neighbor's holiday light

display proclaiming goodwill to all men who have lost their way in
the dark

as they tried to find the car door, the bottle hidden behind the seat,
reason

to keep on going past all the times they failed at sharing love, love.
It's weak they think —

or some romantic bullshit, a movie set propped up behind on slats,
said the wizard

of junk understanding who pretends to be the wise all-knowing dog
behind a cheap fan.

It's in the plan for the new world straining to break through the floor
of this one, said the Angel of

All-That-You-Know-and-Forgot-and-Will-Find, as she flutters the
edge of your mind when you try to

sing the blues to the future of everything that might happen and will.
All the losses come tumbling

down, down, down at three in the morning as do all the shouldn't-
haves or should-haves. It doesn't matter, girl —

I'll be here to pick you up, said Memory, in her red shoes, and the
dress that showed off brown legs. When you met

him at the age you have always loved, hair perfect with a little wave,
and that shine in your skin from believing what was

impossible was possible, you were not afraid. You stood up in love in
a French story and there fell ever

a light rain as you crossed the Seine to meet him for café in Saint-
Germain-des-Prés. You wrote a poem beneath the tender

skin from your ribs to your hip bone, in the slender then, and you are
still writing that song to convince the sweetness of every

bit of straggling moonlight, star and sunlight to become words in
your mouth, in your kiss—that kiss that will never die, you will all

ways fall in love. It doesn't matter how old, how many days, hours, or
memories, we can fall in love over and over

again. The Seine or Tennessee or any river with a soul knows the
depths descending when it comes to seeing the sun or moon stare

back, without shame, remorse, or guilt. This is what I remember she
told her husband when they bedded down that night in the house
that would begin

marriage. That house was built of twenty-four doves, rugs from India,
cooking recipes from seven generations of mothers and their sisters,

and wave upon wave of tears, and the concrete of resolution for the
steps that continue all the way to the heavens, past guardian dogs, dog

after dog to protect. They are humble earth angels, and the rowdiest,
even nasty. You try and lick yourself like that, imagine. And the Old

Woman laughed as she slipped off her cheap shoes and parked them
under the bed that lies at the center of the garden of good and evil.
She'd seen it all. Done it

more than once. Tonight, she just wanted a good sleep, and picked up the book of poetry by her bed, which was over a journal she kept when her mother was dying.

These words from May Sarton she kept in the fourth room of her heart, "Love, come upon him warily and deep/For if he startle first it were as well/to bind a fox's

throat with a gold bell/As hold him when it is his will to leap." And she considered that every line of a poem was a lead line into the spirit world to capture a

bit of memory, pieces of gold confetti, a kind of celebration. We all want to be remembered, even memory, even the way the light came in the kitchen

window, when her mother turned up the dial on that cool mist color of a radio, when memory crossed the path of longing and took mother's arm and she put down her apron

said, "I don't mind if I do," and they danced, you watching, as you began your own cache of remembering. Already you had stored the taste of mother as milk, father as a labor

of sweat and love, and night as a lonely boat of stars that took you into who you were before you slid through the hips of the story. There are no words when you cross the

gate of forbidden waters, or is it a sheer scarf of the finest silk, or is it something else that causes you to forget. Nothing is ever forgotten says the god of remembering

who protects the heartbeat of every little cell of knowing from the Antarctic to the soft spot at the top of this planetary baby. Oh baby, come here, let me tell you the story of the party you will never forget, no matter where you go, where you are, or where you will be when you cross the line and say, no more. No more greedy kings, no more disappointments, no more orphans,

or thefts of souls or lands, no more killing for the sport of killing. No more, no more, except more of the story so I will understand exactly what I am doing here, and why, she said to the fox

guardian who took her arm to help her cross the road that was given to the care of Natives who made sure the earth spirits were fed with songs, and the other things they loved to eat. They like sweets, cookies, and flowers.

It was getting late and the fox guardian picked up her books as she hurried through the streets of strife. But it wasn't getting late. There was no late, only a plate of tamales on the counter waiting to be

or not to be. At this age, said the fox, we are closer to the not to be, which is the to be in the fields of sweet grasses. Wherever you are, enjoy the evening, how the sun walks the horizon before cross

sing over to be, and we then exist under the realm of the moon. There's where fears slay us, in the dark of the howling mind. We all battle. Befriend them, the moon said as a crab skittered under her skirt, her daughter in

the high chair, waiting for cereal and toast. What a girl she turned out to be, a willow tree, a blessing to the winds, to her family. There she is married, and we start the story all over again, said her father

in a toast to the happiness of who we are and who we are becoming as Change in a new model sedan whips it down the freeway toward the generations that follow, one after another in the original lands of the Mvskoke who are still here. Nobody goes anywhere though we are always leaving and returning. It's a ceremony. Sunrise occurs everywhere, in lizard time, human time, or a fern uncurling time. We

instinctually reach for light food, we digest it, make love, art or trouble of it. The sun crowns us at noon. The whole earth is a queen. Then there are always goodbyes. At sunset say goodbye to hurt, to suffering, to the pain you caused others,

or yourself. Goodbye, goodbye, to Carrie Fisher, the Star Wars phenomenon, and George Michael, the singer. They were planets in our emotional universe. Some of my memories are opened by the image of love on screen in an

imagined future, or broken open when the sax solo of "Careless Whisper" blows through the communal heart. Yes, there's a cosmic consciousness. Jung named it but it was there long before named by Vedic and Mvskoke scientists. And, there is

a cosmic hearteousness—for the heart is the higher mind and nothing can be forgotten there, no ever or ever. How do I sing this so I don't forget? Ask the poets. Each word is a box that can be opened or closed. Then a train of words, phrases

garnered by music and the need for rhythm to organize chaos. Like right here, now, in this poem is the transition phase. I remembered it while giving birth, summer sun bearing down on the city melting asphalt but there we were, my daughter

and I, at the door between worlds. I was happier than ever before to welcome her, happiness was the path she chose to enter, and I couldn't push yet, not yet, and then there appeared a pool of the bluest water. We waited there for a breath to catch up, and then it did, and she took it that girl who was beautiful beyond dolphin dreaming, and we made it, we did, to the other side of suffering. This is the story our mothers tell but we couldn't hear it in our ears stuffed with Barbie advertising,

with our mothers' own loathing set in place by patriarchal scripture, the smothering rules to stop insurrection by domesticated slaves, or wives. It hurt everybody. The fathers cannot know what they are feeling in such a spiritual backwash. Worship

boxes set into place by the need for money and power will not beget freedom. Only warships. For freedom, freedom, oh freedom sang the slaves, the oar rhythm of the blues lifting up the spirits of peoples whose bodies were worn out, or destroyed by a man's slash,

hit of greed. This is our memory too, said America. Heredity is a field of blood, celebration, and forgetfulness. Don't take on more than you can carry, said the eagle to his twin sons, fighting each other in the sky over a fox, dangling between

them. It's that time of the year, when we eat tamales and latkes. We light candles, fires to make the way for a newborn child, for fresh understanding. Demons will try to make houses out of jealousy, anger, pride, greed, or more destructive material. They place them in a

part of the body that will hold them: liver, heart, knee, or brain. So, my friend, let's let that go, for joy, for chocolates made of ashes, mangos, grapefruit, or chili from Oaxaca, for sparkling wine from Spain, for these children who show up in our dreams and want to live at any cost because

we are here to feed them joy. Your soul is so finely woven the silkworms went on strike, said the mulberry tree. We all have mulberry trees in the memory yard. They hold the place for skinned knees earned by small braveries, cousins you love who are gone, a father cutting a watermelon in the summer on the porch, and a mother so in love that her heart breaks — it will never be the same, yet all memory bends to fit. The heart has uncountable rooms. We turn to leave here, and so will the hedgehog who makes a home next to that porch. We become birds, poems.

ELENA KARINA BYRNE

Cow Song

For Thomas Lux

I heard them, far-off, deep calling
from behind death's invisible floor door. Their wallow
metronome from the after-rain mud was one giant body.
Arizona's yellow arm's length of light all the way
to my own body standing at the edge of their field held
me. I moved toward them and they toward me, as if to ask
for something from nothing, as memory does, each face

dumbfounded ... dumb and found by
the timeframe of my own fear, surrounded at dusk.
There was a plastic grocery bag, its ghost body cornered
small against a tree, and there was a heavy smell.
Desolation is equal to contained energy now.
Their heavy bodies slow toward me, my own
slow inside their circle without kulning.

Kulning is a Swedish song for cows, not
a pillowcase pulled over the head. Here, the mountains could be seen
from far away. There's an abandoned physics, a floor door,
my own head-call herding me, in-hearing nothing but them.
Bone for bone's female indicates the inside
of the mouth when singing is grief alone and is curved.

You can't stop shifting no matter how
slow. It sounds like confusion in one direction.
I wanted to tell you this in your absence. It sounds like the oak,
it sounds like the oak of floorboards in God's head.

PATRICIA LOCKWOOD

The Ode on a Grecian Urn

Is worth any number of old ladies.
A grandmother hung from a cliff
like a tense moment in an action
movie and the Ode, speaking itself
with its hand on one heart, steadfastly
refused to save her, in fact it did that thing
where it ground each finger out with
a motorcycle boot and then ate
its cigarette for emphasis, whooping;

some old-ass bitch was in pussy church
when the Öde, now spelling itself
with an umlaut, swung its urn
at the back of her head, really clocking her;

till the violets in her church hat grew
from the floor and won a third-place
prize for consciousness;

the Ode is pushing nanas off bridges,
detonating them with dynamite,
tying them to railroad tracks with
squeaky young rope, pouring big glugs
into them out of the skull-and-crossbones
bottle, the Ode is checking
its pocketwatch, which points always
to death-to-old-ladies o'clock,
it is shrieking UGH YOU'RE LIKE ONE
HUNDRED and YOUR BREATH SMELLS
EXACTLY LIKE HORSE MEDICINE
HO, the Ode is blasting holes in them,
is laying them out in the potpourri
aisle, is stabbing them with those icicles
they always said were dangerous,

the Ode means ill to all
of them, the Ode is worth any number …

and the worst is I believe it. The worst is I will
become one, without having written anything like
the Ode on a Grecian Urn, and sit in long rows
along with my kind, till there the Ode comes striding
toward me, my necessary death at the ready,
my pulse like black grapes at its fingertips,
saying, "Fear not, it will be fast, the forgetting
of great poems will fly through you in bullets";

beauty is truth, and truth …
but already I am losing it,
all I know is that the world is falling away,
and you won't believe what it is wearing,
the ridiculous pantsuit of me, a old lady,
crumpled hopelessly at the crotch,
a flower valiant in its little butthole
— all the vital syllables are being erased —
its space-age fabric now seen for what it is:
an embarrassment, my name is turning
into Edna, Myrtle, Dorcas, my descendants
find my peppermints disgusting,

the urn is approaching to scatter me
over a landscape that is heaven on earth,
and in the feet of the poem I am running
— in mad pursuit, and struggle to escape —
chased as if I am worth one million,
Pearl, Opal, Ruby, Coral,
until I am caught by the feeble arm,

and because it is true I am telling
the Ode: you stood in me like a spine,

put poppies behind my eyes,
just the fact of you, that he took
one raw spring to set you down
instead of going out to tip heifers,
tweak noses, or sexually harass
huge curvy vases, you were for me
too, though they would trade me
in all my Beulahs, have lined me up
to enter that land in my turn, you let me
memorize your most satiny parts
and repeat them in hospital waiting rooms,
first to myself, and then almost out loud,
mine, mine, the world's, all mine,
something to say in the face of tall sickness
as I quietly try to unwrap hard candies,
as I tug down tissues from my sleeve,
because it is true I am telling you, Ode,
that I had a throat and you boiled in it,

and the Ode is murmuring almost gently,
"But do you like my ending?
Some people don't like my ending,"
I don't, I never did, I thought it was
so overwrought,
though now that I'm here myself why not
if it has to be this way
then better
put a bright red cough on all that white

Jewel Thief Movie

I was so happy in the gem room.
The sun was president, I was just
dug up, all hell had shrunk
to a sulphur crystal. Something danced
on the point; it must have been me.
I had a hundred faces, and one of them
served up the ceiling in a perfect slice —
like a twelve-year-old saint
in some countryside where they only
read Revelation. I had some small
nugget of sense, for once, I was a mind
that understood the light ...

Rain rained in my aquamarine.
The world's knuckles gripped the bedstead.
I felt the red dynamiting of me in Missouri,
where all outdoors was my candy store,
where color sucked at its all-day self
and never became less sweet, less
new. "I want to put it in my mouth,"
said someone, "I almost want to eat it ... "

I had dozens of uses, but I was mostly
flat beautiful. Visitors just gasped
in the matte-black room where I freely
fluoresced. They saw me laid on a dictionary
to demonstrate my transparency,
which was complete; they could read the word
everything through me.
My name meant blood, meant seawater,
meant lemon. The eye in my agate
never blinked. I was believed to be formed
of frozen moonlight. I was cut so that a star
shone back. The purest and wind-clearest
hunk of me they carved into a horse.

When I was split to the purple and somehow still
standing, they called me a cathedral.
Yet just to the left of that
I spilled all over velvet.
The velvet is what did it —

I wanted to be smuggled.
Wanted to ride past all the alarms,
just before that drop of sweat hit
the floor. Wanted to end up in god-
knows-whose hands, a heist.
"Obscene," said a man behind me,
"just in piles like that ... obscene."
Then I spilled another carat, laughing.
In Missouri you could pluck me

straight up off the ground. Gumdrops,
gobstoppers, jujubes. I thought:
try to suck me down to nothing,
and find yourself up against one
million years. In piles like that.
Just out there. For anyone. Obscene.
The legs of the real thing were
opening, flash and flash and flash.
I said: go ahead and smash the glass.
Give me a break-in like a kaleidoscope.
Someone will entirely drip with me
as soon as I get out of here.

RICARDO ALBERTO MALDONADO

Morning Is Morning

I have some explaining to do — 5 o'clock
meant I would speculate
about artichokes (Greek) and the unfarmed mackerel.
Anyway, the men would present us with a bed of carrot
and potatoes + 1 cup of broth.
Our husbandry in sharp mustard
suit, laden with trial pieces for the fondue. I would prefer
not to. I had such friends —
a long time faring all through the West
with my filth and a bouquet of cutlery
where I had put it: by me.

And yet expansive, the things made by the things
I made. And a supervisor hovering behind me. The heaviness
of being.

I am the Name, Jehovah called from the bush. I had visions
of pigeons. And I replied:

Here I am to be called Ishmael and beget.

DOROTHEA LASKY

A fierce and violent opening

Blood is gushing everywhere
From the lips of the bear's face
Out the elevators
The children's eyes
When they are taken down by the ax
The whole hotel is overtaken with blood

You know I've started to think
You really shouldn't say
Things you don't mean
The way you gushed into me
And then that woman
Who seems so much older, and isn't

Dear woman, I read your essay
That fate could have been me
Blood is gushing from between my legs
I can't feel a thing
No really
I can't feel a thing

When they propped me up
They said, oh, she's so strong
But I am not
I cry too
I cried for you
You left me, always, in the rain

Dear love, you were so brave
The blood exploded within you
You were that whole hotel
Could have been us
I gushed
Out came the blue-green cream

The ghost

I saw him
His body a very pale sea, almost green
Soaring above me in a different sphere
With gold wings
He had a blissful expression
One maybe he never had
Certainly he was always smiling, somewhere
When he died
I had just gotten betrayed by a friend
I thought was mine
I forgave him
Was more just said
You live through any of it
But what is the red shoulder we long to see
I thought that I too would reach a great canyon
My arms and legs blissed out
Instead I blossomed inside
Oh I loved his wife and children
But they were still here with me
When my father died he went straight up to heaven
When the ghost died he stayed with us for a while
I forgot to mention that the wings were gold and green
And the winds were heavy
They held his body
Afloat in air as if in the ocean
I forgot to say that when it was summer
I too measured the red bell heads
I said the hell with it
All of it
Heavy air will you hold me
Suspended in the ocean of time
Where I will never see you again
My skin gold and green
Sweet king, you left us
I know it

Dark is dark
The darkness, darnit
It surrounds
With heavy air
Arms and legs suspended
The head

The Clog

What stays in
Doesn't come out
Nipples hard with milk
When things are of another time
They are of that time
Not timeless
They are no longer here
Nipples hard with liquid or falsities
White and soft
I can't get it out
No matter how hard I yank
Or pull and suck
Face watching with my own
Nipple in my mouth
Like the room she's in
I went and I seduced
But no matter what
I couldn't get her to leave
Aqua and in the morning, coffee
The bathroom gold and green
No matter what I said
She stayed there
She had her own fantasies to wait for
Milk that never comes out
It grows inside
Does it fold back in time
I want to say it becomes different
The man who grafted another face
What poems I wrote for him
No I want to say
That when you came at me
With the syringe
That I loved you
In gold and green
You came at me

Revision upon revision
Of your love
It wasn't like you
To give up
I knocked and knocked
And you went back
Into your doorway
What days
The nipples rising
With future things to come
What happened to those thoughts
To those people
I loved that woman
In the building
Sunset road
The place
With the dead babies
But no matter what I did
How hard I yanked
She would never leave
I knocked and knocked
No matter what I did
Or said
I just couldn't
Get her out of there

KARL O'HANLON

From "In Memory of Geoffrey Hill"

The day glared, breathless: an eye socket.
Clouds barely shifted, and the opal sky
was sheared into dry-dazzling millions.
Yet fall in, the sky, it did not.
The mail did not go undelivered,
dogs were walked; lovers fell savagely
out of and in love, and all between.

Seven concussed days, his draft longhand
swaying like supple pillars of gray flame,
erasures; in the long nights his desk lamp
revealed the window streaked with chalk
sweated off the fen, which was England.

Once Ribera's Jacob, now Jerome,
Ugg-booted at the piano, "The Irishe
Dumpe" from the *Fitzwilliam Virginal*
hindered by the little lion kneading
his lap. Later, the papers howling
of guignol ambush would milk
his delighting spleen as the rectory
self-veiled in evensong and dusk.

Somewhere over an inexpressive sea
of rain-sleek tiles, the contemptible
perfection of gardens, perhaps up
from the weird moonlike muteness
of the Black Country's broken kilns
and felt absences, it came winging.
He died without dread or pain.
A sour storm rides the Levant,
rinsing the domeless yellow streets.

On the steep road to Worms Ash
the coverts take the tincture

of foxgloves, where the shade
of Housman, deadly-formal kink
still running through him, fidgets
among the cinder-like moths.
Hill makes his way to Pisgah.

ANDREW McMILLAN

martyrdom

tonight   I started walking back to you father
it was meant to be a stroll but then I started
walking faster   father   I started chanting all
the names of all the men I ever went to bed
with   father   my thighs were burning and my feet
were heavy with blood but I kept the pace and chants
of names up   father   listed them to fence posts
and the trees and didn't stop and started getting
younger   father   and walked all night till I was home
just a spark in your groin again and told you not
to bring me back to life   told you I repented
every name and had freed them of me   father

ALISON C. ROLLINS

Word of Mouth

After a Nick Cave "Soundsuit" made from buttons and found vintage abacus

When George Washington became president in
1789 he had only one tooth in his head, a single
premolar poking up from his gums. His dent-
ures were fashioned from lead, gold wire springs,
brass screws, the teeth of humans and cows, elephant ivory, and hippopotamus bone. It is a myth
that he had false teeth made of wood. A mis-
perception put forth by those misled by the hair-
line fractures that ivory and bone possess. Just as
cherry wine will stain cloth with a rust-hued vein,
Washington's fondness for dark wine blemished
his teeth. The fractures eventually darkening, until resembling the grain in a piece of wood.
The darkening of fractures is rather curious.
The makeup of the flesh, the constitution of
origin, the trackers of bloodlines thrown off
the trail. It is difficult to determine what discolor-
ations have tunneled their way through the body.
Spider veins climbing the back of my legs like a
winding river mapping the trauma. An unspoken
collective of ephemeral bits and bytes, suffering
most eloquently preserved in the mouth. The skin
of one's teeth decides many a fate. A black woman's
incisor settling down inside a white man's maw.
Overall, a quizzical look, an off-color joke about
progress, the very blood a trick of the eye, an ocean
blue on the outside of the skin, a blushing
red if viewed just beneath the sheath.

•

A tooth is made up of the crown and the root,
all the King's Men destined to revolt. There are

many ways to worm your way inside, many open-
ings in the body of an animal. Some orifices gated
with white entryways. A wooden portcullis, a pick-
et fence, a laced corset secured tightly by a maid,
a pointed geode just waiting to be pulled, the cavern
wall glittering in the dark. Sharp crystals ornament
the cave's jawbone. *Cave canem*, quite naturally speaking. A hooded hole a place for some to hide or go
seek. A toothless whistle the signal for the slave
hunting bloodhounds, with canines fanged like
water moccasins. The swamp mud gushing like
the suppertime mush sloshing between the gums
of a Confederate soldier. The terror of limbs at
odds with the self. In World War I, trench foot
meant frequent amputations, the blade sliding
like floss between each toe. Some diseases attack
the foot or mouth, gums left inflamed in the
cross fire. A grieving mother wears dog tags
around her neck. Her son's baby shoes and teeth
cast in bronze. The pulp at the center is how the
tooth receives nourishment, how it transmits
signals to the brain. The forgetting makes the
present tense possible. Memory is the gravity
of the mind. All the icebergs have started to
melt, milky objects left hanging by a
string, the doorknobs means to an end.

•

The keyboard's toothy smile splayed wide,
the flatlined cursor blinks impatiently on the
screen, my fingers struggle to tap into word
processing. I monitor all of the track changes.
Even the computer is a slave to death. Its in-
nards already bygone, its body obsolete upon

year of purchase. I am a librarian, swimming the
digital divide, my predecessor's paddles —
a mass of floppy disks in an office closet.
They pile up like the teeth of slaves waiting
for sale. An affluent businessman at the door,
his hands panning the saliva for white gold.
His fingers parting the cavity, pursed lips cooing,
I need something of yours to call my own. The desire
to chew and smile at will. My grandmother lost
her mind before her teeth, lost the memories before the enamel gave way to rot. My face has my
mother's abacus features. We are, in fact, diphyo-
dont. In one lifetime we develop two sets of teeth.
The missing space filled with air, a hollow exile
before the native tongue. I pray my unborn child
will have a gap. What the French call "dents du
bonheur" or lucky teeth. The womb's peephole is
rather impressionable. I will fasten the buttons of
time. I will take the baby's body in my own,
whisper a plea in its discriminating ear:
Try to keep your wits about you, my love.
Memory is about the future, not the past.

LINDA BIERDS

Lepidopteran: A Cento

Lines and phrases by Vladimir Nabokov, Alan Turing, and Thomas Hardy

In ... the whitish muslin of a wide-mouthed net,
in time of the breaking of nations,
and in elementary arithmetic,

the lichen-gray primaries
keep in sufficiently close touch
as to impose one part of a pattern onto another.

The vibrational halo
of the string figures
passing from flower to flower,

border to border —
night-moths of measureless size,
circling

among the young, among the weak and old,
hawk-moths at dusk
hatching

the war-adept in the mornings —
the vibrational halo
near the great wings

is not the judgment-hour,
only thin smoke without flame
written on terrestrial things.

I confess I do not believe in time.
And the highest enjoyment of timelessness
is an imitation game ... filled with

the mysteries of mimicry ... But
when a certain moth resembles a certain wasp
and a deadly cipher

flaps its glad green leaves like wings,
what is our solution?
Peace on earth and silence in the sky?

I think that is not
the faith and fire within us ... Still,
I look into the depth of

each breeding-cage,
each floating-point form
cleft into light and shade,

hoping it might be so.

The Underwings of War

National Pigeon Association, England, 1940

Notch.
Web.
And then,
down the shaft,
lesser wing coverts
and marginal coverts, and soft,
greater underwing coverts — although never as great
as greater under-primary
coverts, gray-coated
and down-plumped,
trailing
what
might
reveal
a pattern
just over the down
that might support a secrecy.
Launched from double-decker buses, or attic windows,
or the dark roofs at Bletchley Park,
the lesser pigeons,
always first
to find
the
fray,
sport black
metallic
canisters strapped to
matted lapel feathers. And tucked
inside, like Russian dolls, a cipher's hollow chambers —
down and down, a Fibonacci
spiral, a paper
nautilus
of words

and
codes
and keys
that shift with
each decipherment.
The bard is in the wand — read space
as shape, read *a* as *i* — the key takes subterfuge,
that doubling, double agency
when tomfoolery
is crossed with
rage. But
these
are
simply
carriers,
word-burdened, instinct-
tossed, searching for the perch within
a blasted atmosphere. Find forms, the message says, and
everything will fall in line.
The bird is in the
wind. The loft
is in
the
smoke.

MARIO MELÉNDEZ

The Messenger

She took the words for a stroll
and the words bit the children
and the children told their parents
and the parents loaded their guns
and the words wailed, howled
slowly licked their blind wounds
until they fell flat on their faces
onto the bloody earth
and death came then
dressed in its Sunday best
to stop by the poet's house
and call to him with desperate cries
and the poet opened the door
not knowing what had happened
and he saw death hanging from its shadow
and sobbing
it told him, "Come with me
today we're in mourning"
"Who died," asked the poet
"Well, you," replied death
and death extended its arms to him
to offer condolences

Future Memories

My sister woke me very early
that morning and told me
"Get up, you have to come see this
the ocean's filled with stars"
Delighted by the revelation
I dressed quickly and thought
If the ocean's filled with stars
I must take the first flight
and collect all of the fish from the sky

Translated from the Spanish by Eloisa Amezcua

JACOB SAENZ

The Bachelor Watches "The Bachelor"

I sit on the couch & witness my life
projected on a screen — I am white
w/a chiseled, dimpled chin & no lips.
I'm a farmer who lives alone in a loft
& not a lowly office worker who lives
w/a roommate in an apartment where
dust balls decorate the floors & walls
& the ceiling rings w/children's feet
running back & forth like baby bulls.
I am crazy enough to be a contestant
on a show where I'm contractually obligated
to propose to a woman who believes
in a heteronormative, patriarchal
idea of what a family should be.
At the end of every episode, I offer
roses to those I wish to make out w/more
& take out on prepackaged romantic dates
I could never afford on my bachelor budget.
For example: a date in a castle, a glass
slipper prop, a clock winding its way
down to midnight. My date & I sip
champagne, chat & eat, then we dance
to a live orchestra led by a maestro
who wishes he were dead. A giant screen appears
& plays a clip of a live-action Cinderella movie
w/Prince Charming played by an actor
I've seen slaughter & behead a soldier
like clipping the head off a rose.
In real life, my dates consist of dinner
at Burger King where we dine on chicken
fries & don paper crowns for a royal feel.
On another show date, I take two women into South
Dakota where we fly over the heads of white
slave owners carved into a sacred Native mountain.
At the end of the date, I offer no roses to either

woman & abandon them on a canopied bed
in the middle of the Badlands & take off
in a helicopter to provide the cameras
an aerial view of wilderness & despair.
At the end of the show, I find myself proposing
to a fertility nurse in a barn made to look
like a chapel & not the place where I raised
my first horse, fucked my first goat. Here,
I will milk the cows for our future offspring
to drink straight from the teat like I did as a kid.
The show ends & I rise from the couch
& walk into the kitchen. On bended knee,
I reach for a bottle of beer deep
in the back of the fridge, pop the top
like a question & take a swig, cold
& crisp once it hits my full lips.

IAN POPLE

Rain

A lexicon of words that were not
said in childhood, and all of those
that were, were said beside
an upturned boat, lapped
planking of the creosoted shed,
were said into the wind on
tussocky ground, by farm-rust vehicles.

The buildings I could not complete
without my father's help, the wind
in which I was at sea. Rain blooming
in August that moved the land
and over land toward the autumn,
sliding through the gates of summer,
feeling for the bone inside the wrist.

A. R. AMMONS

Finishing Up

I wonder if I know enough to know what it's really like
to have been here: have I seen sights enough to give
seeing over: the clouds, I've waited with white
October clouds like these this afternoon often before and

taken them in, but white clouds shade other white
ones gray, had I noticed that: and though I've
followed the leaves of many falls, have I spent time with
the wire vines left when frost's red dyes strip the leaves

away: is more missing than was never enough: I'm sure
many of love's kinds absolve and heal, but were they passing
rapids or welling stirs: I suppose I haven't done and seen
enough yet to go, and, anyway, it may be way on on the way

before one picks up the track of the sufficient, the
world-round reach, spirit deep, easing and all, not just mind
answering itself but mind and things apprehended at once
as one, all giving all way, not a scrap of question holding back.

**FROM AN OPEN MAP: THE CORRESPONDENCE OF
ROBERT DUNCAN AND CHARLES OLSON**

DALE M. SMITH

Introduction

The following selection of letters appears in *An Open Map: The Correspondence of Robert Duncan and Charles Olson*; a separate collection of lectures by Duncan on Olson will be available in *Imagining Persons: Robert Duncan's Lectures on Charles Olson* (both volumes edited by the late Robert J. Bertholf and myself, and published by the University of New Mexico Press, December 2017).

Duncan opens this passage of letters from Majorca, where he and his life partner, the visual artist Jess Collins, lived for a year beginning in spring 1955. Duncan's June 1955 conversation focuses on the dynamics of form and friendship ("kind and kin," as he phrases it). Later in August, Olson draws on German naturalist Ernst Haeckel (1834–1919) to make a formal distinction between individual creative transformation and cultural change. This is in response to Duncan's comment (quoted in this selection by Olson) regarding "the sign as image not symbol." Their conversation is grounded in a diverse creative nexus of historical imagery, Romantic poetics, and the morphological specificity of Olson's interest in the history of forms.

These selections suggest the large range of ideas and reference points throughout the correspondence, and they show how the development of Black Mountain poetics took form not only within literary contexts, but in much wider frames of cultural reference.

•

Letters by Charles Olson and Robert Duncan are held at the University of Connecticut in the Charles Olson Research Collection in Archives & Special Collections at the Thomas J. Dodd Research Center. I am grateful to Dodd Research Center archivist Melissa Watterworth Batt for her support in the preparation of the letters.

Mary Margaret Sloan and Christopher Wagstaff, the co-trustees of the Jess Collins Trust, offered kind support of this project and permission to publish Robert Duncan's letters to Charles Olson. Thanks also go to Elise M. McHugh and James Ayers of the University of New Mexico Press for their aid in the preparation of this selection of the letters.

Banyalbufar, Majorca
June 19 and 21, 1955

Dear Olson: We arrived this afternoon after two magnificent & miserable days in Barcelona—magnificent because of Gaudí and the Catalan museum, somehow I was unprepared for what the fact that all of Pedret and Tahull were there would mean—these churches aren't the product of Medieval princely wealth, like the pure splendid gothic cathedral of Palma, but of native imagination—the frescos, fragments of which, or amazingly all there of which, rescued from country (and then *pagan*), mountain churches, from their ruins. Romanesque then, but pagan. Repeat the word and set the eye for what the world-contempt, terror, and giantism means. Faces hunger. Or where there are smiles, Madonnas that are idiots, with Child, face emptied into?; and on capitals, the starkest terror I have ever seen, in a sacrifice of Isaac and then as one changes, walking around the capital, a terrible jubilation. The Scapegoat! But the animal is in the first tableau, innocent, before the idea of sacrificing him. Isaac lives, because his innocence is sacrificed. Give up the innocent animal, and save the man! And then out of that what We all are. And in Gaudí again, which is 19th century neo-gothic, this time not pagan but the other outlander, ourselves—or in the sense that we might be like Mallarmé, and Darwin, and Bergson, outlanders. And I've begun to get some notes done on Gaudí from that trip. Oh yes, and "miserable," that was the fact that to do even this we have to budget it, count it out, allow for it, and then exceed visible what we can afford; and then we had open deck passage and it raind the day, and turnd just at evening so that relieved we could make it.—The Creeleys are here for this week, and then, too soon, he will be gone.

6/21

How does this business of kind and kin go? I write FOR A MUSE MEANT as a letter to Denny [Levertov] because it was through her work that I was seeing that the mastery of walking lay in the mastery of stumbling and then how to fall! upon which it was all built (as only a dancer, thru an art, learns to fall): and receive a wounded cry that I am ridiculing her work. Then, out there, Corman writing to you that the poem was ridiculing your work, or a satire, or a parody; and your letter to Creeley with me there biting at the heels. It's how this business of kind and kin goes that dogging my own heels (who else is it that includes H.D., Stein, Zukofsky, and dada in the pot—a reading of the text might have cleard up who the particular was); but of the kin that Denny or you were unprepared for it. As Addenda Denny's letter to me, my reply to her, and your letter to R. Creeley illuminate the poem, and poem illuminates them. It would be this that would make it all clear. And back to kind and kin that the work gets under the skin, bites, demands no easy realization. So, my reading notes of *Maximus* are propositions for the poet, and from this, for me and then you write "it is made for the poet himself!" and the particular is then you. But a poem, like a map, or the record of a science (read, Harvey's *Circulation of the Blood*), or the witness of a religious man (the accuracies of St John de la Cruz) are written for the man who is concernd. The hot air of "the critical era" as the critics call it, is that these Schnorers and So Fharts suck up to everything that doesnt concern them. Men pawing over Lawrence and Blake, professors I.B.M.ing Pound—that breed!—who have no regard for the process. What can they verify? They see the pome like the real estate dealers see a map. By what analogy can they read at all.

Let's set against that, and then to see it, your record of discovery thru Melville, or Lawrence's *American Literature*. Then back to these letters, as I take sights on Creeley's prose, or you and Denny take sights on "For a Muse Meant" … it's not our understandings, or discriminations that makes it: but the adherence.

Well, then here is our goddamnd language, or the Anglo-Saxon way of hiding his concern with it, keeping it "unsaid," or surrounded by words pointing without distinguishing: "kin." But we are left with "love" and "in love" to say it out with. What is the verb of "eros"? Only the way of talking shows it, then by mimesis not by naming, and no verb, the language must move as the passion of it does. The word "love" is anyway demagogy of the Xtians. And it is in service to Love that loving is realized—a *virtu*, not a virtue; just as it is in service of the Poem, the Conception, that making or conceiving is realized. Your poem *LOVE* relates to *POEM*—the sense of the appropriate, create and/or avoid, is of measure.

> The joy for me of Charles Olson, or Robert Creeley, or Denise Levertov is the joy of the work and its visibility, which we also call the work. Old Whitman wld call us companions. Here's where we will re-see the Christians, that there

was the idea that "The Church" was a commune (those who communed??). What is shared is voluntary, a voluntary.

But there it is — a kind of "love." Or the friendship of the Friends. The "thee" belongs to it; the "thee" which the English, and then the Americans, hide away, or tremble before. (I feel even here, trying to keep my distance, that to speak of it is to trample all over it.) But without this kinship a man's life is hell. The particular hell that Lawrence's life was, he who wrought all friendship not to the test of work shared but to the test of sexual coherence, to the touch. But how the hell was his "self" to be touchd without those paroxysms of outrage, those "noli me tangere"s, that necessity, that must go on to exceed this line of tensions to oblivion. To overcome the nervous irritations and convulsions of "knowing." Consider the difference between the sufferings of Melville as it comes to us as we love him thru The Work, they flower in the being embodied, in The Work ((And it seems to me that the love between man and woman is likewise when it is embodied in the Child — the companionship there in which the pleasure or pain is not all redeems. As Lawrence who wanted the Coming to redeem — who does not conceive of the Child — suffers the intensest sense of the Otherness of the woman. Unintelligible emotional pain takes the place of the intelligible pains of labor. Give birth to me! give birth to me! he cries to Frieda. Thou shalt give birth to no other.

But this Child I am talking about is, like the Poem or the Love, a desire, a vision, of whom the child is the persona. "The Love," "The Love," "The Love" it is all the dramatic embodyment for celibates, homosexuals, and for lovers, who live for themselves or for each other; or for world sufferers who live for others. What can they address? for the Second Coming.))

Well, then the differences between the Melville in his work; and the Melville as he tried to tell Hawthorne about him Self, or as he sufferd his domestic scene. (How did I circumnavigate that parenthesis.)

A man pleading to be understood, or proud to be recognized, or guarding his secret. And so covering his sexual organs that sex might be his secret. And thus must speak of love.

The whole process is a lie, Williams sez, unless, crowned by excess, it breaks forcefully, one way or another, from its confinement.

What goes with Creeley you ask? I see it anyway like that — that it's got to do with Ann, and with, is it a process or a confinement.

————

————

Well, old continent straddler, I'm trying to get at something. And no matter how I goes about it it sounds like I'm putting someone down or setting someone up. But I means these, Melville, Lawrence as exempla. Of what it was like. And when Creeley comes in, it's because it was his story as he told it to me that, or as he has told it clearly in *The Gold Diggers*, or the poems, that brings What Is This Thing Calld Love, as the song goes, into mind. And there it goes chugging away at it. It needs a novelist to put this sort of thing straight out, complete, clear. Poetry, or short story, tackle another thing about it.

Old Man Mose you are with your stone tablets.
For me, the desired extreme is that the form be made in the air, or delivered up to a forgetting ear, or written, at best, on paper on its way to the fire. I mean, if I went mad, this might be my madness. A lucid sense of what the word is made actual.

This after an evening arriba at the Creeley house in which talk of what's up went in circles. There is only one established factor = Ann is going to America in October or November in order to settle into more of her estate. And there is a dual variable factor: she wants a separation, or maybe she won't. In case of Creeley solo he has no money to make it here; and he faces the problem of where and how to get a job and take hold. In case of Creeley familia, it must go as she allows or as she wills. A snarled yarn of economic, domestic, amorous, erotic, sexual, ego, aesthetic, etc. etc. motives and conflicts of motive. And dont ask this tired old psycollegeizer to turn on his wisdom as such. Smother a sphinx in goodwill butter? Cut the life-line lest it be an umbilical cord? Drag the rich man thru the eye of his needhole? Me? R. Bovary Duncan, fix the old foot with instructions from home?

Yrs
Robert

And yrself about ready to, if only etc., get up from out under the old Black Mt. Vulture, Mr. Prometheus, lineman?

•

Black Mountain, NC
August 21, 1955

ON DUNCAN ON
THE PANTOKRATOR

ego sum lux mundi

(1)

a city is a sign of that
the many have it too

polis is a happening
to be together to avert

> (1a) Sticks/ and against which sprays
> from the myrtle bough:
>
> avert.
>
> And produce. These
> are the injunctions, the hand
> held up.
>
> The cornucopia,
> the great bodied spirit I

She eats the young
by preference

and the riddle is late.
The first thing is,

there isn't any answer.
The trouble with a sheep

> (1b) "This goddess crownd with the
> walld imperishable city clutches in one hand to her breast a miniature
> lamb — in time we see her again holding the miniature child-lamb.
> What have any of us who aint shepherds got to do with this thing?
> Something, some insistent thing, because the images bring back ?out
> of memory? the sheep"

is that we aint allowed to be

                              (1c) "as the lion, bear, hyena, horse
and elephant rise up into feeling from their jawbones"

She has a sister.
The sister went down into hell.
She was stripped of her garments piece by piece, stage by stage
of her passage. When she was admitted to the last hall, seven
old men looked at her naked. And her sister
sneered. She packed her off back to earth with all diseases
after her. Woman is two.

(2)
luz
es fuerza
                              (2a) " .... the throne
there is measurably   the book   the light"
no good other than
that we would   grit keres bacilli fistula:

                                    the pipe or reed from which
                                    the infection comes

                                              what terms?
                                    what *terms*?
                                    "great wingd many-eyed seraphim"?

I believe
in the distraction. The meanings
have not changed — the strength
of all / the polis / the light.
The things have.

              In the fistula
is the music, is where I stand
on the seventh sphere, look

(look! she is there!

              At the Pillars,
Mendes hidden in the thigh

like a fish-hook,

flesh   and the proud

       (3)   No book.
           We have no book.
           We can sit as he does,
           and spread our knees.
           But there's nothing on it.

           A word is a speed
           which fuerza hath,
           happen the great bodied spirit is

           The book
           is what we make

           (3a) "a like wise complex iconography"

That is: (1) *animals* (surely you are right that sheep are not for us non-shepherds; and I'd guess that what the images bring back is not the Lamb for you but
(2) *earlier sizes of oneself*, exactly, *bambino*: that you put the sheep & the City Madam together is where giantism first asserted itself *literally* on any one of us ((it is of course very boring, once one knows that another discrepancy of size is more interesting: Troilus, on the 7th sphere — or those fat thin long stupid swelling retina images which overcome one before sleep once in a while, that vertigo

(((A Note at this point: why animals? I don't much take phylogeny here, except in the sense that in the psychic you move the whole system of Haeckel's law forward, that is, the phylogeny is the history of the individual as his own limited species; and ontogeny is the present stage of the movement of sd individual (in the sense that each new instant is a form of birth or development of the further organism: Whitehead's "actual occasion," to reinforce the point, that the past-future-present is no more than the matter & total of, at the outside, 1/10th of a second.)

Animals, like flowers, are the only possible companions size-wise when one is small. I had a guy Cabbage (of Mephisto Freud!). Etc. Anyone fill in their "companion."

But that don't end it. That's the recalled picture. The *action*. Think of it! The owl howls in the night. The dog bites. The automobile drives you into the gutter. A red flower. The sour-grass you eat. What a population is being bred for the city....

     And ma (and pa?) govern, sd city. Are kings and queens. Are Pantokrators!

   You will note I avoid or evade all later transformation. Again, I suppose, the reductive process: find out what the objects are on which the words run to place a name, and to which experience runs to set the place, to see here is where he she it (each man gives his noun, until he knows the proper noun!)

I take it we cannot miss the proper noun (the likewise complex iconography) once the world (mundi) (urbe) is re-inhabited, is constantly (permanently) inhabited: no distraction. Experience is not distraction it is the amassment of the materials of recognition: one does not know a new thing one knows what one knows. This is very difficult.

     (((I am cribbing, here, from yr wonderful statement in yr letter to Creeley this week on having it all, not as ego, but as man, having it as wide and handsome as you damn well can:

to recognize, I dare say.

    I am struck (or stuck) by the cluster: that all later experience goes home, is centripetal in the sense that it bombards these hidden clutched *earlier* animals & selves
        to release them
         And that size
(later permanent formal size, the pressure — of the eyes, in Giotto, of the sitting, in yr Pantokrators (the "terror & majesty") which no "piety or luxury" can throw down, can dethrone)

comes when those creatures are
named & placed.

Ok. I begin to repeat myself. It is stupid. You and I have
no argument. You *reduce*, willy-nilly. And produce, what is more. It's
wonderful.

My love & admiration,
Olson

•

TO ROBERT DUNCAN

Black Mountain, NC
August 24, 1955

Robt (Sunday) — thinking more abt yr letter, & the partiality of my
answer as poem.

That is: was able last night to confront the poem
with a psychological examination of it (and, incidentally, as a result,
though I didn't look back at the text, the Against Wisdom thing, especially the speech is fire stuff).

And tho I value such an examination as no more
nor less than any other technical aspect of a done thing, I was led to
see that again I was pressing on you (as I had in the Wisdom letter &
piece) the reductive process as one to be held to so that a "like wise
complex iconography" may come to all of us ((such as certainly you
marvelously achieve in the Venice Poem — St William Shakespeare!)).

What struck me in yr letter, was the way the prose
sentences on the two interlapping waves of the Barcelona things (the
City Madam and the graffiti of the animals as the object of the hunt,
whether paleolithic or 12th century scratchings of knights & horses)
was, in fact, reductive: that is, that what invoked you was those ener-
gies (fuerza) which you at that moment are.

And that the lovely lines pivoting
on the two churches (La Bons and Tahull), and the Pantokrator, are
productive, by displaced rhythmic activity as well as displaced iconography (using displaced in both instances in no pejorative sense at
all, au contraire, as transformations.

But my question persists: when is a transformation possible to the reductive materials????

Ok. Just to say it that flatly, to further the investigation (mine perhaps, not necessarily yours at all, but we are such damn brothers, or at least i know you are brother of mine, so vividly and surely do you so often invoke me, and, by resistance, a person stands up inside me like the eidolon of Patroclus over Patroclus himself, his chariot and his grave!

And to see this image (idol).... have you noticed, by the way, the crazy etymology of yr word icon and this one idol? That they are both the thing seen, the sign ("you will see a sign").

And the sign as image not symbol (I again battle that modern word, and cry that symbology is when the form has stiffened, and that only image-icon-idol is intensive, only when the things seen are presented in that first vividness does one have form, that asymmetrical classical thing.

Ok. Excuse, please, the last aestheticism. Not at all interesting. I come back to that damned word reductive. Makes sense. Break it down. Get the pieces. Work from them. Have no intention but oneself as the possible source of the transformation: that if one *honestly* (wow!) tries to make the picture, the picture will be iconographic — will be whatever is the polarity of reductive: (productive? reproductive?

You will now see (as I do! why I make as much of *eidos* as you do of *eikon*:

it's crazy, because it comes out the exact opposite of what you are so exact that 12th century had, giantism.

I guess I am arguing that the little, parvo, eidolon (the brother) is what we are made up of: that is, that the person has size (the Pantokrator) as any one of us *is* an assemblage of the essential little persons we are made up of. — (It is apposite to a sense of kin or tribes you may have seen me also refer to. I take it, of course, that what Ortega y Gasset called life as no more than preoccupation with itself is a fucking intellectual statement which leaves out its activeness: that preoccupation must lead to the dynamic of *recognitions* (naming, like the poet sd

                                        (& locus, or placing, as I
keep adding:
            what,
                        & where?
                                ubi, et
                                        qui

And I need not labor to you of all, that these places & persons as
things & spots are all inside any one of us, that the whole world & all
experience is, no matter how real, only a system of metaphor for the
allegory (Keats called it) a man's life is.

What I don't think is sufficiently known (as anciently it appears certainly to have been) is how *limited* (& thus how big) is what we *have*
to *recognize*. (Why I speak of kin: that the circle of the bee-hive or
omphalos of any one of us is a closed circle which opens solely when
the inhabitants are *known*, that there is no *out* until the *in* is done.
                        And that the *practice* (I use it in the religious
sense) is permanent (both as to duration & to intensity, that is, that
the very persons & places sought, are *permanents* too, that the matter
& the means are one, and are in both time and space.
                                I dare say that is why I no
longer fear the static: that stasis is not the lack of movement, it is on
the contrary the recognition of movement as it is molecular or atom-
ic (to speak as in the 20th century) in the comparable sense to which
an agricultural people spoke of the Year, and divided it into two, the
Pankarpia was it and the Panspermia or something, the spring & the
fall:

(((I have the urge to tell Robt, in the pile-on of his troublings over
Ann etc., it takes a year, Robt, it takes a year at least! &! Imagine!))))
Such agri-
                                        .... culturalism!
"a standing still": "To stand."
                There is a Pantokrator (Byzantium?) in which a huge giot-
tesque Christ as father holds a Christ as son-baby (also giottesque)
on his lap (no book, I think) — and on this chest is an amulet (3rd
dimension) of the Holy Ghost (as dove, I remember): an exact dis-
placement of the feminine. And size (gained? at least *got*.

And you know what I think of the Omaha,
and the practice of the signature animal from the adolescent dream
(yr lion, hyena, elephant, horse.
I am puzzled as to how much I take it
the psychic is also recapitulatory. I think i take it very much, if the
20th century's revision of Haeckel's law is let in: that ontogeny can
just as well *create* phylogeny.

CONTRIBUTORS

KAVEH AKBAR's full-length collection, *Calling a Wolf a Wolf*, is published this month by Alice James Books.

ELOISA AMEZCUA* is an Arizona native. Her debut chapbook, *On Not Screaming*, was published by Horse Less Press in 2016.

A. R. AMMONS (1926–2001) was the author of nearly thirty books of poetry, twice winning the National Book Award as well as the National Book Critics Circle Award, the Robert Frost Medal, and the Bollingen Prize.

LINDA BIERDS's ninth book of poetry, *Roget's Illusion*, was published in 2014 by Penguin. She teaches at the University of Washington.

ELENA KARINA BYRNE's latest book is *Squander* (Omnidawn, 2016).

ROBERT DUNCAN (1919–1988) was a central figure of the San Francisco Renaissance and of the Black Mountain school of poetry. His collected poems and plays appear in two volumes with the University of California Press.

ROY G. GUZMÁN* is the recipient of a 2017 Minnesota State Arts Board grant. Born in Tegucigalpa, Honduras, he will pursue a doctoral degree at the University of Minnesota.

JOY HARJO has published eight books of poetry, including her most recent collection, *Conflict Resolution for Holy Beings* (2015), and a memoir, *Crazy Brave* (2012), both published by W.W. Norton. She was recently honored with the Ruth Lilly Poetry Prize from the Poetry Foundation.

TERRANCE HAYES is the author of five collections of poetry, including *How to Be Drawn* (Penguin Books, 2015).

MICHAEL HOFMANN has translated work by Alfred Döblin, Hans Fallada, Franz Kafka, and Joseph Roth. His new book of poems, *One Lark, One Horse* will be out next summer.

DOROTHEA LASKY is the author of five books of poems, including the forthcoming *Milk* (Wave Books) and *ROME* (Liveright, 2014).

PATRICIA LOCKWOOD is the author of a memoir, *Priestdaddy* (Riverhead Books, 2017), and two poetry collections. She lives in Savannah, Georgia.

RICARDO ALBERTO MALDONADO* was born and raised in Puerto Rico. He is managing director at the 92nd Street Y Unterberg Poetry Center and cohosts the EMPIRE reading series with Hafizah Geter.

ANDREW MCMILLAN's* debut collection, *physical* (Jonathan Cape, 2015), was the first poetry collection to win the Guardian First Book Award; it also won a Somerset Maugham and an Eric Gregory Award.

MARIO MELÉNDEZ* received the Municipal Prize of Literature in the Bicentennial of Linares, Chile. His poetry has been translated into many languages including Italian, Arabic, and German.

ELIZABETH METZGER* is the winner of the Juniper Prize for her first collection, *The Spirit Papers* (University of Massachusetts Press, 2017). She is the poetry editor of *The Los Angeles Review of Books Quarterly Journal*.

TYLER MILLS is the author of *Tongue Lyre* (Southern Illinois University Press, 2013). She is editor-in-chief of *The Account*, teaches at New Mexico Highlands University, and lives in Santa Fe.

ROBIN MORGAN has published six books of poems. Her seventh collection, *Dark Matter*, will be published by Spinifex Press in 2018. She is the recipient of a National Endowment for the Arts grant in poetry.

KARL O'HANLON* grew up in Purdysburn, County Down. His debut pamphlet is *And Now They Range* (Guillemot Press, 2016).

CHARLES OLSON (1910–1970) was a dynamic force in post-World War II American literature. His essays "Projective Verse" and "Human Universe," with the epic writing contained in *The Maximus Poems*, defined open-form poetics beginning in the fifties. Works by Charles Olson published during his lifetime are held in copyright by the Estate of Charles Olson. Previously unpublished works by Charles Olson are the copyright of the University of Connecticut Libraries. Used with permission.

IAN POPLE's* *Saving Spaces* was published in 2011 by Arc Publications. He teaches at the University of Manchester.

ATSURO RILEY lives in San Francisco.

DANA ROESER's* most recent book, *The Theme of Tonight's Party Has Been Changed* (University of Massachusetts Press, 2014), won the Juniper Prize.

ALISON C. ROLLINS was born and raised in St. Louis city and is the Librarian for Nerinx Hall. A Cave Canem fellow, she received a Ruth Lilly and Dorothy Sargent Rosenberg Poetry Fellowship in 2016.

JACOB SAENZ is a poet living in Chicago. He currently serves as an associate editor for *RHINO*.

EMILY SKILLINGS* is the author of *Fort Not* (The Song Cave, 2017). She is a member of the Belladonna* Collaborative and splits her time between Brooklyn and Hudson, New York.

DALE M. SMITH* is a poet, critic, and editor who lives in Toronto, Ontario. *Slow Poetry in America* (Cuneiform Press, 2014) and *Poets Beyond the Barricade* (University of Alabama Press, 2012) are his most recent publications.

COLE SWENSEN* is the author of seventeen books of poetry, most recently *On Walking On* (Nightboat Books, 2017) and *Gave* (Omnidawn, 2017). She teaches at Brown University.

ROSANNA WARREN's most recent books of poems are *Earthworks: Selected Poems* (American Philosophical Society, 2016) and *Ghost in a Red Hat* (W.W. Norton, 2011).

JAVIER ZAMORA is a 2016–2018 Wallace Stegner fellow and a 2016 Ruth Lilly and Dorothy Sargent Rosenberg Poetry fellow. His first book is *Unaccompanied* (Copper Canyon Press, 2017).

* First appearance in *Poetry.*

Woodcut of Jeffers by Barbara Whipple

The Robinson Jeffers Tor House 2017 Prize for Poetry

We are pleased to announce the 2017 Prize Winner and Recipient of the $1,000 Honorarium

Donald Levering
Santa Fe, New Mexico
for his poem
"The Notebook"

Honorable Mentions, each with an honorarium of $200, are awarded to

Justin Hunt
Charlotte, North Carolina

Mary Pinard
Roslindale, Massachusetts

Cynthia C. Snow
Shelburne, Massachusetts

Chelsea Wagenaar
Valparaiso, Indiana

The annual Tor House Prize for Poetry is a living memorial to American poet Robinson Jeffers (1887-1962)

Final Judge for 2017: Eavan Boland

See www.torhouse.org for poems and membership information
The Robinson Jeffers Tor House Foundation
P.O. Box 2713, Carmel, California 93921
Telephone: 831-624-1813 email: thf@torhouse.org

THE LONDON MAGAZINE

Est. 1732

launches its first ever

Essay Competition 2017

1ST PRIZE: £500 | 2ND PRIZE: £300
3RD PRIZE: £200

Opens: 1st July
Closes: 31st August

1,500 words only | non academic essays

thelondonmagazine.org

POETRY FOUNDATION
SEPTEMBER FEATURES

POETRY PODCASTS	*POETRY MAGAZINE PODCAST* *Poetry* editors **Don Share** and **Lindsay Garbutt** talk to contributors and share their poem selections from this issue with listeners. *POETRY OFF THE SHELF* Producer **Curtis Fox** explores the diverse world of contemporary American poetry through readings and interviews. *POETRYNOW* September's four-minute episodes feature new poems by **Kiki Petrosino**, **Gerard Malanga**, and **Ana Božičević**. Produced in partnership with the WFMT Radio Network. *VS PODCAST* **Danez Smith** and **Franny Choi** host a bi-weekly series where poets confront the ideas that move them. Produced by Daniel Kisslinger and presented in partnership with Postloudness. Podcasts are available free from the iTunes store and on poetryfoundation.org
HARRIET BLOG	September's featured blogger, **Christopher Soto**, discusses poetry, craft, and the writing life of a poet at poetryfoundation.org/harriet.
POETRY FOUNDATION .ORG	View essays, interviews, and a new animated series of contemporary poems retold as short films for all ages created in partnership with **Motionpoems.**
EVENTS	Plan your trip to the Poetry Foundation in Chicago to see some of our September events! *Poetry off the Shelf* **COLLABORATIVE WORKS FESTIVAL: MYTHS & LEGENDS IN SONG** Wednesday, September 6, 7:00 PM *Poetry off the Shelf* **KAVEH AKBAR & CHARIF SHANAHAN** Wednesday, September 13, 7:00 PM *Poetry off the Shelf* **EVE EWING & MARCUS WICKER** Thursday, September 28, 7:00 PM
EXHIBITION	**"THROUGH THE WORDS OF MISS BROOKS" TYRUE "SLANG" JONES MURAL** June 16 – September 22, 2017 Monday – Friday, 11:00 AM – 4:00 PM

P O
E T
R Y

POETRY FOUNDATION
61 West Superior Steet
Chicago, Illinois 60654
poetryfoundation.org